fo

-vus friend

Mike

Cold and sneezy
Saturday night in K-burn.

Death of New York City

Death of New York City

selected poems of
Nina Zivancevic

introduction by
Charles Simic

cool grove press

Copyright ©2002 by Nina Zivancevic

All rights reserved under the International and Pan-American Copyright Conventions. Published in the United States by Cool Grove Press, an imprint of Cool Grove Publishing, Inc., New York.
512 Argyle Road, Brooklyn, NY 11218
http://WWW.COOLGROVE.COM

Publishers Cataloging-in-Publication

Zivancevic, Nina, 1957-
   Death of New York City : selected poems of Nina Zivancevic ; foreward by Charles Simic. -- 1st ed.
   p. cm.
   LCCN: 2002141108
   ISBN: 1-887276-27-0

   I. Title.

PS3576.I5836D43 2002   811'.54
                                  QBI33-564

Acknowledgments
ENZO CUCCHI for all the illustrations with permission courtesy of Bruno Bischofberger Gallery in Zürich, Switzerland

First Edition
Printed in the United States

dedication

to the bright shadows of
H. H. Dudjom Rinpoche
Ven. Kalu Rinpoche
Dilgo Khyentse
&
the warm presences of
Namkhai Norbu
Lama Tarchin and
both the Tertons Sogyal

Sol wa Dep !

Contents

Foreword by Charles Simic	xiii

I. The Spirit of the Renaissance

Spirit of the Renaissance	1
Stained	4
Explained	5
Charges	6
It Was Then	7
Opinions	8
If	9
Sometimes I Dream	11
Diary of a Thief	13
I Feel	15
There is Nothing But...	16
Ash Wednesday	17
Apart	18
Ariadne	19
My Angel	20
Small Town	21

II. Skeches from Byzantium

Skeches from Byzantium	24
Poem with a Tilde	26
Healer's Wife	27
Tristan and Isolde	28
Sonnet for T.W.	30
Talking to Your Answering Machine	31
Florence	34
Roma	36
Venetian Mask	38
Garden of Distress	40

For Aki, Princess Mononake, in a Strange Land	45
At The Frick	48
Royal Chase	49
There are People Who Can Never Talk	51

III. Exquisite Corpse

Exquisite Corpse	54
Camera Obscura	55
Recepisse Poem	57
Only two, and then you	58
What Is It?	61
Gilles Dies, So What	63
Ode to the West Wind	64
They Blame Me	65
Extremes	66
Right Place	68

IV. Death of New York City

Death of New York City	72
If You'd Just Imagine	78
"Dear G."	79
That Happened	80
May	81
Could Glory	84
Notes of Zyder Zee	85
Lonely Women	86
Lonely Men	89
Blood	90
This is it	92
In Philippe's Hospital	93
Lined Up	95
Don't They . .	96

Angle	97
The Real Meaning of Life	98
East Side Blues Again	101

V. Descending the 'Three-Jewelled' Staircase

Love	104
On Death	105
Memory on the Line	106
The Test	107
On Losing Just About Everything I Own But My Life	108
On Nothingness	109
On Impermanence	110
Games We Play	113
Insane	115
Ancient Verse	116
Airplane	117
Winter Song	118
Brave Song	119
From Shahnameh Diwan	120
Poem for All Sentient Beings	121
Instinctual	122
Transparency	123
Rose	124

About the author and illustration credits ... 126

foreword
by Charles Simic

Nina Zivancevic is one of the most original poets writing in Europe in the last twenty years. Born in Belgrade, she has lived in Paris and New York, but the voice that comes through in her poems is that of an exile, of someone who travels with eyes and ears open. The genius of her art lies in her ability to make surprising connections between diverse cultures and literatures giving her poetry a richness and range that is truly rare. She has published many books of poems in her native Yugoslavia and has won prestigious awards there, and ought to be better known in the United States. Zivancevic is an astonishingly fine poet.

1
the spirit of renaissance

Spirit of the Renaissance

Long pink snails of memory
stretch along the shady docks
watch ancient mariners seducing sirens
sleepy on the rocks
oh, the rocks and the docks
and fools playing at fairies
the certainty of a wasted existence in
puffs of flagellated smoke
and charming redheads obeying rituals
green for greed given for candles green for health
superior gondoliers slide past uncivilized shores,
Cristobal Colombo sleeps with an Indian
the pampas turn gold, children in black sand
for the love of sand for the love of sound
sacrifice the language of semblance
and reassemble reseda sunsets.
Oh, the foolishness of hours spent in
the hunting for speech!
Oh, the pomposity of nightingales sculpting
space with their beaks!
Oh, protoplasm of languid summer air,
resistant parks and maimed lovers
protected by their tepid fears
await the help which never arrives

the trains are shut off warriors
who wait for their planes,
turmoiled clouds, the placid and ignorant
wait for purification,
the ill-destined defendants glued to their chairs,
chessboards of time waiting for the sun,
and I was waiting for you
on the corner of two anonymous streets,
your face was real but people said,
"They must be from Paris,"
my nose was bleeding, "It's nostalgia,"
you said, the evening was soft
like a wounded man,
the clouds falling gently like autumn leaves,
the color of ocher embraced as quietly like in
Appollinaire's verse, just as in Appollinaire I walked
quickly, unbecoming like a memory
unbecoming like verse were his hands his
pensive face full of filth,
they built a temple for him in Patras,
a man or a woman—I did not ask, torrents of rain
buried the city, the smell of atonement and ashes
filled the air,
the air was a mountain from within,
it reigned over my skin and was not for a moment
for sale, any second it might have disappeared,

this feeling of anguish and
full comprehension,
"You are great," the frogs and the birds said,
somewhat content, while the cats stretched their
oily backs
in flat disapproval of my words,
I came to Egypt for his funeral,
now it was raining and we could hardly breathe,
a Japanese lilac tree flourished in my garden,
his fingers were abstract, my uncle was very sick,
my onion heart crisp and translucent,
and in everyone's eyes, oh, if we dared
to look into each other's eyes—
the spirit of the Renaissance.

STAINED

You feed me with stained and broken mirrors---
What should I do today?
I always worry
When you are not around
I belong to the sky,
In a metaphysical room
You become ecstatic, you read your books
And I follow, you encircle me
Bring me close to myself, like last night
When I trembled before something hollow
Stirred your vision, you,
Immobile, immortal immigrant
Turned upside down
In my lap.

Explained

Oh, my love is not
Like a red red rose,
It is rather a white lily stained
With blood, it is more chilly
And sustained than mid-winter air,
More hopeful and yearning than
A sudden summer rain, more
Bashful and proud of its own insufficiency
Than an angry child, so,
What am I saying "my love"?
It is all yours!

Charges

If ever I get charged with despair,
Lack of confidence or sloppy emotionalism,
Allow them one look at your bright ribbons and your nostrils
Of satin and your fingers of feathers
Where it all began
The orders I obeyed contained an element of
Truth and freedom to choose
To accept your orders or to ignore them,
I was a slave to you and not to circumstance,
I swore in the light which you endowed me with
Before you took it away,
Radiant, so I could learn a form of darkness
We both could have done without…

It Was Then

It was when Man Zimmer and I
Did not keep each other on a leash
That we had the best sublime congregation
How simple and complicated creature
on the same wavelength trying
To set himself free from himself and from me
Perhaps this is not a story
But has its morals
Two winds meeting
Can cause quite a draft
Just like this saxophone going
To blow this tune away

OPINIONS

I dye my hair blond thinking of Titian,
Mother, I am jealous,
Keith Haring likes lovely dancing boys!

II
When I say that I prefer Ben Jonson
To Shakespeare --- it does not mean that
I had acquired a good taste,
It is just a taste.
And it can shift to tackiness,
Tawdriness being the highest quality
Of our mutual Twentieth century art

III
Mark thinks that there is some intelligence in my work!
Whenever I see him
We end up munching dinner,
So do I truly make any sense?
"More than this. It's always more than that."
(Roxy Music)

If

If only I could have been allowed one moment
Of silence once a day
That would've done me more good than
Any other thing I tried to do/acquire/learn
But I always went for the impossible
And then I kept complaining
That I couldn't get it.
    ~ ~ ~
Once I met a man
Who was so stupid that he was claiming
That he was a poet --- at the same time
He was afraid of abstract thinking;
On another occasion I lived with someone who
Had nothing to do with 'ars poetica' but who allowed
My silence to grow. He was such a selfishly generous,
Generously selfish man, I could not forget my life
With him years afterwards.
    ~ ~ ~
The fear of silence with some people was
So great that they kept barraging us with words,
As if they had really something to say.
Those were the poorest creatures I've ever encountered
But I was a coward to tell them that.

Once I was so threatened for my life
That I started speaking incessantly. It was then
That I started performing in theater which like magic
Finally liberated my soul.
~ ~ ~
Once I loved a man too much — my fear
Of losing him was so great
That anytime I approached him
I had to utter a million words, which he despised,
To which he laughed with contempt- the strangest thing
Though is that, due to my words,
I never 'lost' him.

Sometimes I Dream
(for Elio)

Sometimes I dream of you,
When I was a small girl I always wanted
To hold onto something like your hand.
Something quite predictable, and then leave,
return, pick it up from where I dropped it.
The last Cantos make the first one,
like in an old Dao,
Like another winter after yet another spring.
I thought you vanished some time ago and I wrote
A love song for you—when people read it now,
they say "Wow!"
Your eye was my camera one September as we
walked past New York City ruins
and a telephone, a common denominator for lies,
that winter, birds were falling dead,
but you said
"Please, believe me," and I thought I could. Then,
you started obeying Thanatos once more,
and I almost liked it.

Oh, I have always loved you because it was
So easy not to, but for the effort
That kept our bills and veins straight, perhaps
We could try to live in the woods
Raising dreams like cattle
No clocks to melt inside us,
The tremendous momentum of thunder
Smooths the days
When I think of you

Diary of a Thief

I. Kleptomania
This morning for the third time
I come out of the Boulder County jail
Snowflakes glued to my lover's pale face
Our fingers touching, no remorse,
Our-Lady-Of-The-Flowers stench in my nostrils,
Balls of fire bouncing in our heads
No coke tonight ---
I should've been brought up in the country!

II. Scribomania
Barred monkey sitting in his cell
Wishing a single piece of paper and something to write with,
Wishing I could say what is on my mind, and it is
Mostly the regret that DeKooning's paintings are
Someplace else as well as my friends, including Creeley,
Who says that the actual scope of paper
Limits your expression, well,
All of them, so far away

III. Megalomania
Mountain peaks under fresh snow
Jack and I barefoot, sick with
Bourbon and too much sunshine.
Foggy mists above Sue's cabin,
Sudden warmth catching up with my heart,
As we touch heavens better than the Concorde
I take home to New York,
Still high, pale blue sky

IV. You See
Denise takes her wolf out for a walk
And still distant from California, I dream
Of white patched earth, 2000 miles of an undeniable
Desire to hear his voice calling me "Zee", reading me
My horoscope in which we never meet,
over the phone, this morning

V. Claustrophobia
Scattered clouds, seven below zero
Plus or minus indeterminate jokes concerning
Mozart's Sonata in D minor, and blue jays taking off
On my mind, less dirty than Villon's notebook,
More innocent than Lana Turner's pillow.

I Feel

I feel quite angelic, quite warm,
Quite soft, quite frightened,
Typically Catholic (the way Vivaldi felt
When he wrote '4 Seasons', at his optimum)
My legs quicker than the Transit Authority,
Simply lit October sun,
I don't need a jacket nor a smile
To wrap myself with
And everyone who sings a song
In the street
Is my brother

There is Nothing But...

This foaming ocean, this sustained
Breath dressed in blue, this vague excellence
Becoming worn thin and overwhelming...

There is nothing but this clear thinking which
Gets demolished by writing it down,
There is nothing but this painful memory of
Foaming ocean and all its births and rebirths,
Contained in this painless foam,
It sprints high and gets low, like life itself
Going on in myriad of circles,
Unless the spiral strikes us and tricks us
Into the bottomless magnitude,
Pumping up tedious air
Which is someone's hobby
Gossip of stars across neutral sky
Which meets the horizon every evening
Splashed purple and then
Makes love to it.

Ash Wednesday

And then he says: everything should be
SO beautiful (beauty being a limp, tepid
Word for the rest of our
Negative emotions.)
And then HE says: I don't feel
Very well, it's February --- a mating
Season for dogs and cats, and then
He says: Don't touch me,
I will never see you again,
But then she says: Probably, I think,
And what I THINK IS crucially
Important for everyone and then he says:
I love your thought patterns- they are
Pretty amazing! And I say: it's all right.
(So much anger and hurt and inward blindness
just because I think in spirals,
and you, in squares.)

Apart

Under your fingers you hide
The infinite and the fire is
Checking the flow of elements in and out ---
Strength of the iron man belayed by water
And his grace—defined by the circumstance
In which he dwells.
Sometimes we become soft like a pomegranate,
Sometimes we are eager to fly. What lifts us up
Above the ground is the force
That binds us to good soil and the air,
So we raise our heads above an avalanche
Of public events: sturdy, black and tangible
They pull the strings of
Cosmic unity together
And apart

Ariadne
(the belated thread)

I was waiting for you
at the edge of a garden,
when I saw you coming from the distance
with someone else and you were smiling,
such a nice evening, indeed,
you said, and she smiled back
then frozen lilies
blossomed on my palms
and a sudden death like a wind
penetrated my heart.
You took my hand and asked: Shall we walk alone
wherever you want?
And it was then that
I knew we could do
each other in
and without

My Angel
(for Francois Lardeau)

My angel is built of strong will and soft colors
his skin of liquid has no remorse
as it lures me to oblivion
his hair of light chestnut smells of
the Tuileries in autumn
my angel has nothing to do
with bad moods and sorrow
I placed him on the sarcophagus of all
my extinguished desires
his fingertips are soft feathers which remind
of someone who used to be me
his thin ankles retain the winds
through which music speaks.
My angel is the catcher of my brusque thoughts
so I have to finish this poem quickly—
he smiles at it without even seeing it—
I cannot do anything for or against him,
but his intuition forgives me all

SMALL TOWN

There was a small town—seedy look
on everyone's face
there was a girl taking pictures
at a subway stop,
oh, she is doing this and
she is doing that, and a husband's
frightened expression at discovering
a moment in which his dear wife smiled
at someone else—this is just
a photograph—she did not want
to take your soul away,
the aborigines built up a totem-pole,
a mysterious temple to worship a goddess,
and then a star and a human being full of vice
and incredible digressions, but then
she stepped right into the dimension
where all sorrows melt
into a turpitude of endurance where
the memories of the world become
fluid and old
and gossip just a cleansing diet
and something you're living for.

2
sketches from byzantium

Sketches From Byzantium

It was
and definitely still is
a man's world,
I said as I watched
a 50m² long jail, with latticed bars
and golden fountains with thin blue enamelled
hamams where the royal concubines used to live,
die and make their sad intrigues,
create perverse gossips, clandestine lies and
cherish their claustrophobic desires under
that all-turquoise sky with magic 'bulbuls'
and sweet sweet smells of amber and the sea
outside, far beyond their reach, their ghostly
desperate love-knots at night
when they sought pleasure or perhaps
just a little tenderness, with eunuchs
or one another, in one of those 500 languages
they spoke coming from different Ottoman provinces
and European countries…
"Je t'aime, ti amo, I love you tonight
but I hate the smell of wounded vindictive epics
that Sultans cast on us." The first feminists
must have been born there where the feminine
was denied with such brutality
and cruel disrespect for anything human

but something pleasurable and shivering
like a Turkish delight, something awfully slow
like a rat's poison, something alluring:
"I also watched the Sultan's fifty-seventh wedding
through the barred lattice window yesterday, and
the poor thing, the Emperor, was clad in brocade
and silk and waited for his most royal viziers,
the bribed little counselors who wished his death,
ach, such is the quality of friendship," a concubine says,
coming out of a bath, stretching her long plump
milky body covered with varicose veins because she
does not exercise at all, and whatever you make
out of it, is worth a story, my friend Kemal
tells me six-hundred years later, while driving
his car up dirty 'caldrmi' road, at top speed
and with Donna Summers booming from his radio;
strange girl you are, he says,
to live in New York City, you had to be born
in Turkey among very few potatoes
with lots of gravy, with a special flair
for distinct personalities, of a brain
filled with hope…

Poem with a Tilde

I feel sad and serious
like little Doña Infanta entrapped
in a Velasquez painting, watching
my silly royal entourage with distant
and soulful eyes, bending over
a ray of light focused on young princes,
niños and dueñas, brushing pearls
from my solitary shoulders, hiding their
friendly deceptions in my curls,
waiting for my dwarfs and pleasant servants
to bring me a casual cup of chocolate…

I feel sad and serious as if I sent
a fleet of explorers to search out
a new continent, to bring me back fresh
spices, gold idols and a new culture,
the exaggerated insults of foreign kings,
soft robes and unusual toys shaped like
a bleeding human heart, but what they brought me
instead were barbarian shells, symbols of strange Gods
with hollow painted mouths,
all trying to speak something simple and awesome
which recalls a whisper, resembles a howl

Healer's Wife

She sits quietly
waiting for dawn,
she is a restless sleep, she is a cuckoo's song,
she is the lady-in-attendance to
someone's crystalline heart,
she, the crystal herself,
reflects dark light
from the depths of all sorrow,
mirage of stumbling pain, she
absorbs sustained miracles, delayed deaths
and successful cures, a cure herself she
hardly moves, her silent lips tremble
her long hands touch the one-who-tires
from seeing the sick and the fleeting
all day and all the same,
to her it seems larger than life to watch
him breathe her breath
in and out as she sleeps
recovering his dreams about the distant
provinces of sky, as she,
attentive, keeps his heavy hair
from falling into his nightmares
of hermeticism, where she
takes off her clothes and closes her eyes
once every thousand years.

Tristan and Isolde
(for Enzo Cucchi)

The red and gray and black
and I cried so much
when I boarded a train
and forgot my coat in Rome
as there was a lance in a Velasquez painting
and a diagonal bridge between two worlds
and there was a battle
between me and you and the worlds we belonged to,
and there was a dwarf and a little princess,
and there was a sword and a gay hero,
and there was a fish and the Adriatic sea,
and there was a swindler and a child inside you,
and there was your tragic grimace of a Byzantine hidalgo,
and then you said: My friend, I know you exist
somewhere and that makes me happy
—and you looked at the painting,
the pavement in Rome and then you said:
Such a lousy city! and you allowed me to be wise and old
and hold you by the strings of my celestial laughter,
my language was fresh and when you touched me
I almost swooned, I got the disease—they called it

Tristan and Isolde, you were lonely and had
a little niño, age 4,
you did not say a word
but your eyes had the color of a disturbed man
who was selling his sadness for a million dollars,
wherever I went I saw your eyes hanging in the
museums of modern
art, some women were crazy about your artists
were jealous of you,
art dealers were happy to see you,
but my fate was to keep your disastrous dreams
away from the rough soil where you slept
if you ever slept, but you never disturbed
your scientific brow with such equanimities as
pain, rest or cruelty,
I lived on your shoulder
and you thought it wise
and you held me close, like an
open orange on your palm
just for once

Sonnet for T.W.

I am not a tinker, darling,
and I should not repair you
-- I just want to spare you
some truths I say ad hoc

When people don't expect to hear me,
my checkered mind goes asunder
before I make a blunder
and feel the way I feel today:

cerulean blue with honey melon yellow
with tints of veronese on the aquamarine ground
smeared with pale dove light

changing tones to burnt sienna
blushed with parma violet – and then I see,
the canvas hardly holds a portrait of you!

Talking to Your Answering Machine

I am sorry I am not able at the moment
to answer your needs and
meet your demands because
it is exactly 6 o'clock Friday afternoon and I think
they are going to spill Acid Rain over China
and kill the Governor of Bhutan Sikkim and Trinidad
and if you do not know what to do
with yourself please do not
kill your neighbor
he is as vicious as you and
all your relatives are baking
a beautiful song shaped like
a chocolate cookie trouble
whose snooze was the booze
for people who are a little loose,
oh, but if you come back home
before 2 and it's almost half past 17
please call me back and forth
I am surprisingly in quest for truth
dying my hair black and am dying to hear your message
although we are fully aware that the General and the
Surgeon
have determined that such words are sheer nonsense
so please I love nonsense
give me your brain massage

you oddly remind me of someone who I don't want
to meet
and he is someone who says:
I am a little bit messy too
but you are his private zoo, can't you say
Boo boo this is
nothing new but you
just tend to ignore my messages
so I will play a cute song for you:
LET'S GO! THERE IS AN OPENING
at 34 West Broadway AND I DO NOT WANT TO SEE
YOU NAKED!
is my microphone there!? Hi, can I get
a drink as red as the left
signal on your malted cheek?
WHO IS INTERRUPTING THIS CONVERSATION?
What did you say? We haven't been talking to each
other
ever since we met, who are you
damn it, you are turning me

into a stripped spaghetti package
as I spin around your something
which is as huge as…
it is a formulated popcorn stand as you sit on it
watching my head turn channels
its screen is empty
I am full of your messages we had enough
of this game
the importance of saying the right thing
here and now,
and the bird says: Hi! have a nice day too!

Florence

Getting up early, feeling nausea,
getting up early under an old green Gobelins hat,
rushing to the city of deadly poisons,
leaving the city of lagoons, miraculous glass
Venetian Christmas beads behind,
walking through the dog shit, leaving the feeling
"Sarebbe, devi essere mio" behind,
dark city with an emblem of lily, dark city
with a pharmacy where Dante's house used to stand,
rushing through the city where Giotto was merciful
to leave his frescoes behind, walking through mud
where a woman, fearing walls, claimed that they had ears,
walking through the city of fears,
running through the city of poisons under my green
Gobelins hat, playing with lily-white marble there where
a word
should be, drowning in the Arno of fears, for indeed,
one who entered this place could no longer find an exit,
walking along cobbled streets where the flea markets

have fleas which crawl up Renaissance trees
and walls of yellow mortar, who might be hiding
there now?
Behind all that mud, mortar and chocolate,
who is left to make a dream?
Walking through the capital of white lilies and
fragile leather,
walking down its poisonous streets
of lilies, of soccer, of pink linen and witty deceits
walking through the city of Middle Aged streets

Roma

During my third day of stay in Rome
I started speaking Italian and wrote verse in terza rima,
the cypress trees stretched above me and Via Apia
Antiaqua,
and in the morning I went to the Hipodromo to find
a stone which speaks of
Caligula's love for horses
and then ate lunch with someone I truly loved
who was a Roman and beautiful, like one of those
fallen centurions (but was married now and had three
children, one of them named after me), and then
I went to Villa Borghese to walk among Bernini
fountains and numerous other petrified creatures,
I had coffee there and it was almost evening,
the trees were still above me and sweet southern air
caressed the Roman balconies and pizza houses,

the home where Ariosto had stayed in March
and April of 1516 is now a hotel;
soft breezes kissed my hands as I walked
toward the People's Church, a girl with a young
and painful face played the organ and
Ave Maria lingered
above Caravaggio, whose St. Peter looked like
an old man
evicted from his low income housing project, and
Baroque angels
hovered over my head as I listened to music
even more innocent than those angels above
and it was almost deep purple midnight when I
gathered my soul and walked down the Spanish steps
into an Anemone sight.

VENETIAN MASK

And he, finally having a good time,
is going to hear eternal Vivaldi at La Fenice;
the city of glitter and glass rejoices
in the cold November sun. And the waiters, so different
from those of Vienna who lit our cigarettes,
always at hand, handy with tips, but these are not!
The Venetians collect their tip before you enter
the restaurant, which you had no choice but to enter
because
it is pink and gay and so close to Don Juan.
The city of Venice does not offer itself
to a casual mind—
quite restless and ruthless it is less
casual than it appears tonight
as I visit an auntie who is one hundred years old,
who became the city itself and who says:
Go to the theater tonight and put some perfume on!

I walk through the city dusk where the young Venetians
in patrician clothes walk their patrician shoes
up and down the Rialto bridge, and the cats, as
Pavese has
already noted, well, the cats wear their fur the color of
flowerpots and watch everyone,
and the flowers
watch the red balconies, the last souvenir
remaining from the Arabs turned Spanish and Byzantine,
but the Venetians hide themselves behind a
carnival's face,
their tribe's past is wrinkled,
their smiles are decorated
behind a mask of gold rust, black and red.

Garden of Distress

I
"Pay all dues to the City"
he said, in your prayers pay
all dues to the invisible, because
who would know, perhaps some ghosts
of well-being were not
entirely satisfied with your stay
in this or, indeed, any other city
which disliked Tsvetayeva too,
this morning, a wake up call
or a play of two small kids
who brought memories of Starwars
and fresh cornflakes—
my son trying to calm me down
Don't worry, ma, you ARE a JEDI
And I am safe with my grandma
And papa's here and pepe Jo
They try to be wise, the five year old said,
These young ones are truly smarter than
Some old friends from dancing halls
Who altogether stopped dancing…

II
'The bells ring without reason and we too',
T. Tzara said in the moments of his tightest desperation—
In the region where dreams sleep,

The kingdoms of anxiety open their gates
At the back of my poetry horse
I ride through them slowly
Thinking of all the silky moments
When I loved this city
So much like you love
A bride who never really belonged to you
And a blond woman, heavily made up
On trains, and the casual
Phone call that one gets for brunch
On Saturday morning
So that Saturday becomes
Filled with restless hope
And then you move
Inside your parlour, snugged with
Computer programs and
Tuna fish sandwiches
– fast Saturday soberings
– in the city of garish lights

III
As if the lights were there to postpone
The death sentence
I walk through the city sprinkled with memories
and soft rain
The steps of my dead friends and lovers echo everywhere
Here is a corner where Luca stopped on his

bicycle to buy me a rose
And in this hidden courtyard now turned into a
flashy movie house
Elio copped some wrong chemical and then
turned blue
And this is the street where Gera and Julia and I
used to paste
Posters for our divine anonymous performances
And here is the spot where I said goodbye to
Philippe for the very last time—I was walking fast
now but almost suffocated by
The nearest and the dearest and the utterly sublime
which is that
Incredible and insipid glory that this city
held for me
I was the dead but now living
Walking through the light rain
As if I never left and never departed as if
I came to Ellis Island many centuries ago
but as a vampire
Changed shapes and colors

Through the centuries
We never leave places where our
Soul was born and not the body

And the man on his Balinese
Instruments trying to think up
A wonder and probably mesmerize
Two old ladies on orange
Subway chairs and a jaded youngster
—they all hold banners of this decorum smeared
with ketchup and eternal lights

And the dear one, squashed with years
And that mad Viennese yearning
He wakes up with bright lights
Slushed snow and loud synesthesia
He examines my wrinkles and
Terminal worries and tries to remember
The dancing hour at which we met
And soared above the situation

Bygone times and future gags deconstructed
As usual, what a pleasure, he thinks very
Fast, almost too fast to keep his attention
On a subject and a soup at the same time
Events pile up we can
Only leap from one event to another,
From an exam to reality, from the
Mountain top to a wheelchair
And back and who can keep
The track of all this, can I ? Can he ?
In Japanese 'ken' means 'bright saber'
As he cuts the landscapes of pure 'NO'
And mud, winter and snow,
Brilliant ice-skater that I am…

For Aki, Princess Mononake, in a Strange Land

What 9 pm is to a sleeping child
3 pm is to a Hiroshima survivor,
what a mint tea is to a street vendor
the bones are to a DADA warrior,
what misfortune is to a philosopher,
a small dental problem is to a gentle housewife,
what poetry is to the indomitable
a daily worry is to a bus driver,
and yet! A kiss is still a kiss
a cat is still a cat
a lion is still a lion
and a friend is still a friend
—unless we turned the notions
upside down and topsy turvy
inside out   and outside
our will and imagination a humble poet strolls…
Stroll, poet, stroll,
Stroll within this universe
Which is your playground
And your kingdom of death
Move slowly and with ease
For you are the master-puppeteer
Of the prophecies to come
And those doubts that seldom leave
But tear us apart

II
In the City of poems,
How come that no one will plant
A poem at your gate?
How come that night won't
Open to your old heart like
A rose, how come you paste
A cigarette upon your lips
And not a smile,
Oh, a smile, so dear, so precious,
Could it be only kept for
Buddhahood and those
Mortal hours when
The ultimate
Understanding of all phenomena

Washes the gates of oblivion?
How come the colors
Cannot bring back the momentum
Of joyful hours and could
I watch them now only
In a theater?
Oh heart, in a form of dart,
Come to terms with yourself,
You know you could, if you only
Wanted to, you know that you could close
Your petals, open them up again, you
Need not any central heating to create summer,
You need not a magnifier
To look at the blind...

At The Frick
(for Simon)

Which I visit in the darkest
Of my visionary hours, a portrait
Of a young man, serious and elegant resembles you
At your best
That deep wrinkle on your brow
And a mad streak of your Nietzschean eye
As you clean the quiet place that used to be
Our home, feeding the birds,
"the love birds" that don't love
each other any longer
our numberless fights buried
loudly under their green feathers,
their flights in the realm of pure thought
where we once met, so, how
could I ever hurt you, how
could you hurt me, under
the shiny cloak of worldly comprehension
of the essence of human destiny,
human selfishness, human
love, in such a silly
animal kingdom ?

ROYAL CHASE
(after Nizami)

We walked into the garden
With miniature pine trees, casual deer and
Singing fountains: it was then
That I realized the royal hunt was
Going on, scorched grass,
Illuminated manuscripts smeared with blood,
Santours in flame; the clock- you said-
Was turned here 400 years back
And the battle of Kosovo
Shifted in time, with bright yataghans
And mutilated soldiers: the rigid,
The senseless and the cruel ruled
Your garden, my Shah of Shahs,
You had to leave Nizami's garden quickly,
And became a nomad burnt by fame !

I was the last
'Northern province' of your empire
you fought for, my house disappeared
in heavy bombing, the language
of our children sprinkled with foreign accents,
the angels on Christian frescoes
in distant monasteries had lost their wings,
their flights reduced to nightly escapades
to the cover-pages of some dubious
newspapers where EVERY THING is fit
to print, except for our exiled songs
and our daily worries that bear no
official translator's stamp.

There are People Who Can Never Talk

There are people who try to say
Something but then they stop
They censor themselves, hiccup,
Have a general for a wife,
Are afraid of losing their job,
Inhibited from childhood
Would like to get some more sleep,
More food, more love and then,
Well, they would talk, there are
People who glue their lips, keep them tight,
They think they know,
They think they know how to negotiate
Without a single spoken word, they assume they
Are too emotional, they think
They are refined, they say
—others can say a lot they know others
say so little by being that loud,
there are people who believe
that the more they say, the less they are
taken seriously, they want madly to
appear serious, there are people
so closed, they can never talk,
they can never become poets…

3
exquisite corpse

Exquisite Corpse

Corpse becomes exquisite through diurnal vivisection
a grave digger is jealous of people who place flowers on
his tomb,
Madonna becomes pregnant by a low metaphor,
a macho character is impressed by high life,
a dog barks
      at a hyacinth cloud,
a child is happy when you tell him a bad joke,
a man—unhappy after you rob him of sheer illusion,
communal living—it's a necessity that comes with age,
but words!
They get lonely
with no afterthought
to cheer them up!

Camera Obscura

And a lady with a poodle barked:
eya—wof, wof!
And a black guy with a black leather jacket
sang "Baifal"!,
and a man with his camera clicked
Click, click!
and a woman with a gun screamed "I'll shoot
you down," and another one with a flower
smiled at me
and a blond child with a peroqueeet called my
name, and the redhead guy called my telephone number
and asked me "who are you?", and I said,
look, I am a genius,
someone completely lost
and crazy who needs A LOT OF AIR
to breathe,
and a man with a motorcycle pulled my hair
and took me for a ride, and the city
of Paris was so beautiful in that late
Sunday afternoon,
but the motorcycle stopped

and we got off and then got high on hash
and then I slept for hours and
when I woke up I saw the lights of
the city, the fact was that all
these lights dwelled in my heart,
it was a big city and I was at its mercy,
but that was the day I loved it, I had
turned myself into a ball of light,
my dreams were squashed under the boots of time,
and I thought "How lovely, finally
I could have a dream that nothing else
happened to me but only that
my dreams were squashed
under the boots of time," and then I went
to a swimming pool
as if there were something
needed to be washed out.

Recepisse Poem

And do I have to glue on your brow
all the prescriptions filled out for me
so that you would understand
how hard I try to be free…?
I thought freedom was smoking
on a train in full swing, age eighteen and that was
in London, 1975.
today I see that to be free is
nothing but to wake up with a smile,
and that is hard, I can't!
And it seemed so easy!
But they closed that Tube train in London,
and you cannot smoke anywhere but in your
bathroom, while your son is asleep.
I used to live under a Communist regime
but they changed its name to fascism.

ONLY TWO, AND THEN YOU
(to my lover)

Although you
never meant to place
my verse on poetic Olympus and would
rather leave the Muses and their Parnasus
to someone else, this is my poem for you:
—among the war-ridden ruins of Belgrade,
and then through the ghostly capitalist
shine of Budapest, and amidst some more
exquisite and ornate parks of Paris, I had a moment
of samadhi just with you,
and though your lovely head does not
recognize that particular intellectual
rigor so dear to my
heart, and though you said that every
great love you had was obliged to leave you
somehow with disgust,
and though the role of an ethical
teacher does not suit me any longer
since I had my own child,
the samadhi was transparent, green and good—
while it lasted, so no need to break one's heart
and ruin bladder because the Almighty
Segneur of Oblivion covers with thick dust

us all, and especially those who believed
in a moment but could not
digest it, or were not
up to it, as some would
say in your precise
language

II
But who cares for doves
nesting in forgotten castles by the Loire
when daily news tell their deadly stories
about the cities bombed overnight
and the last tender hope for the Great Comprehension
in life was submerged in the Danube submarine yesterday
yes, who cares for the doves but me and you
after we lived through so many affections
and then the last two?

III
I wanted to live in a Bosch painting
and become a sparrow, a sunflower or a butterfly...
My heart was still open and my liver healthy;
I was that black bird soaring very high into the clouds
of poetry—but when I died no one
was there to bury me
and then you took me out to dance;

I never took you for someone else.
oh my Muse of Good Weather, your laughter,
your dainty fingers and your sorrow
indelibly dwelt in me from the start—
when the melancholy hour arrives will you
be there to rescue my wings
from the depths of disbelief and anger,
will you be the one to turn the music on?

What Is It?

And, of course, then—
poetry.
What is it—I cannot really tell
only that I've encountered it personally
on very few occasions in my life, until one day
it almost disappeared from it,
and I knew how sad, how tragic life was,
stripped out, in lack of the lyrics...
Oh, no, it certainly is not a soup of potatoes,
it certainly has nothing to do
with heroic acts of killing and dying,
although it has something to do – with basic instincts
and innocence;
most surely it has nothing to do with grants,
cheap mountaineering, career or with money,
although every so often
it hardly becomes visible without them.
it certainly avoids definitions
and categories thus it hardly could be taught
in schools, it is even rarely spotted when chased after
or pursued with deeds "well-intended",

it certainly needs
a teacher to be communicated
from one being to another,
it certainly needs a person or anything human
in order to be told to, and it surely needs
no one in order to exist
but these clouds and clouds again,
as many of us have already
mentioned long ago.

GILLES DIES, SO WHAT

How should all this enter my 'Baroque' mind?
We avoided another riff, gingerly. Out of an accusation
and into the Christmas shopping.
Three million people
starving in my old homeland and you are still
at ease bombing me
with international politics and Sade's theory
of isolation. Above the tree trunks of our solitude
there is a stable doubt growing, dumbfounded.
Look, I did not move a single inch today, but
Deleuze has jumped out of his window;
all by himself and you
did not help him, either.

ODE TO THE WEST WIND

Oh, great great West Wind,
take me back to all places and people
I cared for, take me away from this
Neoclassical order and dumbness,
away from the North Station where they
took 2,000,000 Jews away to the camps
so only my grandmother got back, take me away
from Europe ridden by plagues and wars,
away from the United States where
people die in ignorance and hunger,
take me back to Serinda where breathing counts
more than action and sublime thinking,
to the non-existent land of poetry and wit
where women don't speak of equanimity and
men dance tango all day long, lift me up
and make me forget this overbearing present,
so, if it is spring,
why am I so far behind?

They Blame Me

Because I decided to trust the unbelievable
because I decided to be calm like a lake
because I wanted to become a breath of air
because I wanted to be alone
because I desired to have so many friends
because I could not be bothered
because I used to sing so many songs
because no one could hear a single sound coming
from my mouth
because Tenzin said, "You always say I,"
because I am I and somebody else,
because no one ever took an interest in my drawings
I had to draw every night
because I believed in silence
I had to write so many words
because I loved so many people dearly
I had to leave them behind
because I disliked the color green I wore it every day
because I did not have to do anything,
I was doing everything
because I liked to explain myself I was telling
every "because", because:
be a cause and not a consequence
because only a cause and not a consequence
has a sequence
because…

EXTREMES

Substantial insufficiencies crawl into my life
close one door behind
then emerge at the exact same corner
where you dumped all squashed dreams
electric fans are hard to get in winter
they could disperse some stale attitudes
as in an allegory, justice is cloaked and perfumed
and walks hand in hand with a fox;
how should I save your manuscripts,
how should I save mine!?
In case something
happened to you or to me,
was the first thought I had
this morning.

II
And why read all these books unless
we learn something new about the essence
of life, human nature, and how to deal with them,
what some of us also determine as 'style',
why keep handsome volumes, lush bindings,
exquisite
ornaments, if their deciphering appears so poor,
impotent
and savage…And why am I
writing these lines to you, my Nietzschean

spirit, ignorant 'dasein',
who despises categories and who
lives in his own Sophist's world?

III
Powerful clutches of human misunderstanding
squeezing my throat in a clench—
along the docks of the Seine and down
the tracks of Paris subway I stretch my
nerves/muscles upright, all alone—
and yet, little Vladi thinks
that life is just a red red shiny truck, vivid and
moving too fast as if escaped
from an American cartoon or from some European
quasi-surrealist joke, whereas we know
that sheer existence is but a balloon
which will take us to the other side
of the shore at the moment when we
neither want to go (there) nor have
any strength to stay.

Right Place

When the timing was right
the moon sunk low into
its red circle
he lifted up my skirt
and found there three 'la cucharachas'
and two memories.

When the timing was right
I woke up late and tried
to be dead serious—every number I
dialed was sweet responsive and promising
just before that bad disillusioning flood

When the timing was right
my limbs were light and supple and I had to move
again to the Kingdom of the Tacky and shiny
and it felt to be good timing.

When the timing was right
you said I was a cat woman
dealing with rats
so I dared not scratch your surface
fearing there was nothing
underneath and then

I was so high there on top of you
singing Dr. John's song "I've been
at the right place BUT IT WAS
THE WRONG TIME"
I've been at the time but,
or perhaps the pace was not
right and was just
an illusion?

1
death of new york city

Death of New York City

They say
maturity and wisdom come with age,
but age does not bring us strength,
rather it welcomes a horrible weakness
of spirit and of heart—it dissipates
our will and makes us blunt.

They say
vulgar thoughts should not be used in poetry,
'emotion'—that's something to keep us alive!
I am alive for an instant and lack
graciousness, that which comes with age.
Is there such a thing as 'poet gracious,' as
a 'poet maudit,' or a 'wild poet,'
a soul to compare to an animal, to a totem,
to a domestic cat?

They say
once alive, souls cannot be domesticated,
or they will die, like being fabricated
in a sex-appeal factory,
in the fabulous courtroom of quick attractions,
mild satisfactions, jovial catering
to sophistication in our beloved City of Doom!

And yet! There is so much room
for every single occurrence of idiocy
in one's own lifetime – providing you have
a life in your prime, a single
effective affection for a Muse,
for childlike adults, wet rooves, gardenias
and book abuse, red hot July evenings
drenched with rain,
oh, she was so plain
and J. went to stay with her...

II
Or, one could see it in the attraction
experienced by Gala when she left
Eluard for Salvador Dali – the legend says
they were standing on a rock,
bare shoulders exposed,
naked arms and their kisses...
Much to Eluard's dissatisfaction,
Gala observed poetry in Dali's eyes,
and there I was, stranded,
unable to produce a single line,
a single thought that was not for you
when you took me to the top of the mountain
and I already had
nowhere to go...

III

And then the young poet stoops
and sits down on the beach
cuddling his blue guitar, singing to the sea,
"I will never get involved, no, not me again,"
telling his story about things noble
and immaculate, and the way 'they really are,'
the youth and his blue guitar!
The irreverent waves wash his song
and carry it to other shores
where elders rest their weary backs
and stuff their sacks with immortal advice
and cute comforts to compliment their misogyny
and the laurel-snatchers with their ladies
of sleeves green and long
as in a medieval song
which I've never learned to sing well,
and then for an instant, I was alive again,
though it felt like living in Hell, but
Virgil was gone, Dante disappeared, Frost
domineered, and the Academies of all my futures
closed their heavy doors to sweet and friendly
whispers (and to those less than friendly),
and sturdy words set themselves free,
repeating stubborn syllables:
Thou Shalt Learn to Agree!

Oh, No! Never shall I 'agree'
with the fact that Marcel Duchamp
made a pact with the fact that he acquired
a patron for the Tarts — from the moment
he set foot on this soil, his new continent,
his talent in the most quivering of all Arts,
of granting his approval to the need
to acquire more and more
        rather than less defined
quasi and refined
        at the Galleries of the Past...

IV
(Return of the Byronesque Muse)

And then the older poet descends alone,
from his outer sanctum and his resplendent, distant sky,
he is here now, all for me and ready to give me a try,
or rather, to try me by showing his "overall" concern,
and if we were to discern his real motive and
his goal from the information which his horns
keep blaring at me
then we could surely understand and agree
on the true substance of 'Poesie' in general
and his significant self in it in particular!

But he, of all people,
does not have to do that!
Oh, I've always loved him,
although he was never meant to
ride over pink clouds through Arcadian dusks with
me—and I was never meant
to write lofty books
on his metaphysics and his
amorous verse which he throws at us so sweetly,
earthly ladies, obeying his
frantic funny formidable rhyme!
No! He should be set free,
and allowed to untie and tie all these
abstract ribbons of my invisible blouse
patched with needles from murky philosophies
--see these tracks and lines?
once he had a love there
but today his shaky hand
won't place me on his sagging lap
--he chooses to think instead
that I'm just a noble trap for his
old man's foot which he
decides, reluctantly, to move
forward
toward me

V
Oh, dear, and how I laughed
and laughed tonight, having all
his thoughts just for me
served on a plate of amusing indifference
and how I remembered all that I lived for
was someone as funny and gracious, though
thirty years younger than he was,
and how we laughed and giggled and sighed
in his car sadly that summer and a little boy
placed between us said, "Zee's so funny,
and so unlike your other silly girlfriends,"
suddenly died in a car accident
like the moment in which we believed
and had something in common, sitting between us,
perhaps that child, or all that giggling
was not enough to keep me happy
through the rest of my life
so that I had to cry a lot whenever
I spotted a similar potential for laughter
and driving someone's car
to a quiet no man's land

If You'd Just Imagine

And how would I feel
if I stood up there before a judge's bench
begging for clarity and understanding,
and I was accused of a second degree murder
of all our plans and hopes, and a cruel officer
kept your eyes closed and my hands clasped
in surprise, and a rowdy lawyer
making things worse,
and you still trying to defend me and take me away,
and a sunny April sky outside,
and then everyone dragging me down to my
inner jail, lacking human sound, unable to hold
my back straight any longer,
yes, how would I feel?

"Dear G."

Unlike the rest, You
should not deceive me, even if
you don't believe my words
such as milk, honey and dollar—
after all, You are such a scholar
and the streets and poplars sing when
you call this quandary "the sea
of living and cognitive truths."
With your mind soaked in January solid
dusky barroom rum, with your Athlete's
foot hurting, I think of ancient Gods
so I give You my wings to put on your sneakers
and you are quite a Hermes when we fly!

That Happened

That happened to Mozart too ---
he dies, and then they discover all his false poems
and librettoes, but on all other occasions
we don't discover
that sort of cuteness in him,
and in fact, one could feel rather
uplifted when hearing his great
flute concerto in B flat
like the other day when I ran out
of breath after seeing Bresson's
photographs, had to seek my father's arms
like a little girl.
"Oh, come cry with
Delvaux's paintings," Eluard once said
under the auspices
of surreal clouds
where too much beauty
meant nothing,
and all

May

SO, please, how does it feel
to wake up in Sleaze
and beg on all these wolves in business
birds in corporations, alligators in
the sewers of New York
to light their polite polish and
flicker their smiles, just for you,
whereas You, gorgeous and segregated
keep your face straight
knocking the stars in and out
daily routine of trodding along a path
your lover designed, just for you
in a fit of immortal anger...

II
And out of your wits and on a rope
of an ultra sheer thread of light
you try to think of tuberoses triangular buildings
wrestling with strange tree tops
which go together with strange trees,
in a strange afternoon in a foreign country...

And yet, a foreigner is not only
a man who seeks a green card or wears a yellow star,
a foreigner could be anyone, you or me
left alone with a bunch of books, taffeta yellow
turnips,
or a sudden wetness on your fingers
you forgot
to whom they belonged
and you have never parted
afterwards.

III
Afterwards it happens
that you move along the docks and melted concrete,
wiping mud from the shoes you bought
in a third-rate store which used to be
a shooting gallery in the lowest side of York,
whispering "is this all, can it be all?" and yet
attentive to a new flow of hopes
oozing from the South
I think of red great Arizona mountains
made of blood black granite and
Mexican flesh.
Nature so generous, so sublime, like

fanciful handkerchiefs in pockets
of bright women
who ended in an embrace of
lonely surgeons operating on their hearts
in their summer offices
    in the country across the Atlantic
on this Earth
which is such a lovely
lonely star…

Could Glory
(for Herbert Huncke)

Could glory erase this sadness
of your face, Herbert,
an omniscient movement of all your facial
muscles which knew nothing
but of fleeting pleasure and perpetual pain?
I lifted my camera and took a shot,
it was a photo and not a needle affair, we did not know
where to go nor where
we came from, one cold
winter afternoon in New York City
where they shoot people, not horses
in the age of Depression

Notes of Zyder Zee

Christmas is here and cards to go,
There is a frenzied woman not letting me
Have dinner with you, and there is D. and
His blond French poodle, there is my friend C.
Fat as usual, there is my sense of fraternity, my ornaments
And my cancelled checks, there are hopes and a need to
travel so far away,
there are obligations which will never stop
Keeping me alive, there is a circus and here is a zoo, there
is a map
And here is an airplane, and also there is Byron's sloppy
handwriting
And his Harold under the library's glass window dying to
escape history
And there is a pedantic Samuel Taylor smoking opium,
and unfortunate Shelley,
And enamoured Keats trying to get away from his disease
and his sense of beauty,
And there is you, under the Christmas tree turning my
miniature
Candles on and off, and an astonished child
"Zyder Zee"
Unwrapping the decorations,
Craving to be me.

Lonely Women

Clenching their teeth
they say they don't care
yes, it sucks to be left alone,
but isn't that how we were born to be?
Lonely women laugh crisply and hear
at midnight their neighbor's cat meowing,
lonely women say: It is His mistake
for He was immature and I was only... A bit insecure
with my art and with my position in this world
yes, it sucks to be left alone
to scrounge   to crawl   to lounge
in someone else's bedroom
and to say: Good bye, honey,
sure we had a good time, please call me again sometime,
nor that I care, but a wee bit of comfort
every human being can do with,
and now I had it for almost a year,
I had it for almost three years,
one of them says, but now I am left
alone again, and my Creative impulse says,
"Hey, don't pick up that
receiver, stay at home tonight,
someone better may call you..."

perhaps it will be him, though
I don't think I'll ever see him again,
he's such an egoist,
no class, none whatsoever,
he REALLY sucks, and the way,
the way he left me, oh,
that really sucked! Were I not
an artist, if I did not have
an ego of my own, it might have been
even worse than this, but tonight
I have no interest in my ego, or in phrases
like, "I gave him the best years of my life,"
"He was my second best, and while it was not
love at first sight…"
on second sight it seemed to me
that we were so attuned, so harmoniously
matched in this universe
no two souls could be more connected and divinely
entwined,
and then, he proved to be what he really was—
a simple swine masked
in lamb's wool, an artistic cape
and portfolio – I saw him for what he was,
and so I was left finally lonely
when he moved out

he left like last night's potatoes
but oh how it sucks to be lonely left alone
to my art and my hobbies,
I couldn't even remember his name
when he walked past
yesterday I only remembered how it hurt
when I made the decision
making decisions always hurts –
and always I've had my own mind
to make them with,
decisions move in and out,
after each decision there is a
better decision to come
and a worse one
after so many decisions no one
feels left alone
Lord, this artistic world such a small lordly
creation, but if you don't
choose your own world someone else might
choose it for you and then leave you all alone
sometimes both of you
choose your own lonely moments
to share with each other and
sometimes
it's just plain lonely.

Lonely Men

They can be bored
and boring, lonely and hurt,
hurt young men trying to determine
their identity, strong or weak,
they are to be taken seriously – the way we soothe
little children – they want
to be in the know, they want to be
in demand, they want to be free –
I say "they" and it sounds like "us,"
oh, but aging men, lonely,
after so many battles are still capable, but are afraid
to show a little tenderness,
they offer stories and bitter eyes instead of
battlefields, so whenever I am
a man I feel lonely, whenever I am a man
I battle myself, and that wretched
part of my ego which wants to win,
whenever I am a gay man I write poetry, whenever
I feel physical I am a young warrior
from the Japanese woods,
and I know, oh, men
with crushed stars instead of eyes!

Blood

Sometimes too thin it was
unable to thicken in your veins,
it carried disease and a stable gene
which refused to stay in one place
it moved constantly from one village to another
was temperamental and killed your
cousin age five was salty and almost
abandoned my body in a green valley
in the country by the sea was
inviting Lamias and their daughters
who wanted to drink it was dark
with anger and visibly flowing
beautiful through marble statues of Greece it caused
my heart to look upon the landscapes of
different faces then almost clear and red,
belligerent fought armies of the invisible
tried to feed it with vitamins and alcohol
was thinking of becoming a sister and a friend
to someone who had the same temperature
and stained my shirt when I placed it
underneath my body was oozing down
the sinkpipe   I took a bath,
left a red spot on his dagger
were his eyes full of this gruesome liquid?
it was vomited in large quantities

my friend almost expired,
generations of artists lived in constant lack of it
it prompted the Hungarians to ride horses
and the French to bargain and play courtly instruments,
some of them decided to drown themselves in old wars
and it became sticky and cold and
maintained a balance in its temporary
frame   it was almost like a movement
in philosophy and
was simply spilled over a girl's vain body.

This Is It

not a poem about the blackbirds
and thunderstorms nor a story which says:
when I and I were together
there were no black thoughts about
stormy weather and the starry sky could not be seen
but was somehow meant. No one
tried to leave stickers on my walls
to convey meaning of any given
transcendental nostalgia
as I posed before a video camera like
so many other relaxed people and then learned
that my heart was so remote from my face
I could almost touch it
(that lively emotion we neglect
in an early morning and say "breakfast").
Breakfast and children and
an accidental friend who confesses
that he/she is terribly tired
of the spinning zoo and the starry sky
and it feels good and God
after you took a shower

In Phillipe's Hospital

Nowadays everyone writes poetry;
I was doing it before I discovered
That fiction was poetry for the adults.
The newcomers spoke of Celan and Holderlin
I was hoping that once they mentioned them, they
would attempt to write like them, in vain!
A nurse stuck her black curls inside the room
And spoke of cold and high temperature,
So many years swirled by us, we did not drown
In our maze of memories and cozy souvenirs:
Instead, you complimented me on my dress, that
Lacy little nothing which would
make Justine blush
In a more enthusiastic situation.
But we were in a hospital where the doctors gave
You only three days to put up with polluted air
On this planet contaminated with wars and basic
Lies and misunderstanding.
You kissed my hand.
As any true cavalier, gentleman
Would do on such a formal occasion—
as if you asked me for a dance but the invitation came
too late! I had to go

And kissed you good-bye with that scent
of heavy rotting flowers lingering in your room
with a number 55 on it.
You thanked me for everything I did for you,
For each and every friend I've had in the past
But could not revive no matter how hard I tried—
the final "adieu"
To the days of my youth was spoken and
I was sobbing
For that part of myself which I wiped off
my fingertips once I remained
Alone, in a cancer ward that last day of July.
My tears had nothing to do with you
Nor with people who wrote great poetry.

LINED UP

They were all lined up
As if they had something important to say,
As if they had somewhere to go!
(Staten Island pigeons)
And if you stared at me instead of
At the Statue of Liberty, it's only because
The more transparent I grow,
the more cryptic I become,
or as Neruda put it "I loved her, and sometimes
She would love me too." Well, I don't know
What happens in summer --- only one
Certainty in November's fog: biting at this
sandwich, sliced ham, Swiss and lettuce
The first one I ever got
In this town the way I really liked it
Or cared to like

Don't They...

Don't they drive you crazy when they start
Examining your English accent and interrupt your
Lunar walks upon the surface of humanity
Don't they have something to respect
When they discover that you were thinking
About your own life at the moment they
Were flashing compliments,
Don't they have something to think about
When you laugh at their lies in public
And obstruct the elevators of their will
By saying something poetic?
Grandeloquent mountains are more merciful
Than those who dial your phone and say
"I'm sorry, I thought it was you
who called me this morning, I was not
there to swallow gossip last night–
my story could have had a plot
from an ancient legend
and I was too literal and literary
not to buy it."

Angle

We could view this guy
from many different angles:
we could say he was
a dishonest man, picking people
like apples, or we could say
he was a shattered, sad creature
afraid to face himself, or one could say
he lost his wife and almost his life
so he was casual with all other women,
or one could say that he wasn't thoughtful,
or one could think that he was truly an artist
deceiving everything but his ideals,
or some would say: he was simply a mean male bitch,
and one would see that he was constantly
attached to the air, and I did not think anything
but simply observed him as he was tending to a spider
on his hand, quite gently at the time
when he was demolishing my life under his shoe,
or his word,
and then, he placed a spider on a fine leaf
upon the highest branch and I thought
Gee, this must be someone who is quite
a gentle guy. And he was.
Someone who killed his wife
and almost his life so he was
casual with all other women.

The Real Meaning of Life

A black woman enters
103rd Street station looking
like the Queen of Sheba, with her
gold lock supporters she walks proudly
up and down the stairs—this is her world,
subways and Spanish words, such as "Hola!"
whereas I belong to no world so
I can become one with the world,
my dreams contain strange deities, perhaps
dreams always contain strange messages
though for a long time I was
claiming the opposite,
the obvious becomes a cruel game
when we choose it, trains never arrive
and people walk, last night
across Central Park my heart
was almost murdered, my feet so weak
could not carry me across to another province,
although weaknesses belong to humans, so what
do we do with someone whose face belongs to
Olympus?
Do we say, "Good, my God,
I've never cared for you!" ?

We sometimes become silent when facing
the beauty of the obvious, these mean
untalented remarks and premature actions.
Whatever happened to that someone in Germany?
Probably he walks
through the demolished streets of Berlin,
or is an extra in
a Wim Wenders movie, not dropping names
but appearances, he respects sunsets
and small grievances, he was too tender
and I could not take it—never regret circumstances,
especially unfavorable ones, you may find yourself
gaping mouth wide open in so many situations...

Years rush by and our serene mirrors
become blue and synthetic, we forget
the ethics and treasured esthetics and start
searching for the real meaning of life, like Herod
who began to appreciate dance only when
there was Salome to fall into a trance
and dance for him and dance,
who danced away her chance
to become someone like Cleopatra
or the magnificent Theodora

(oh, poor starving women of the Lower East Side,
oh, poor starving women of Turkey and North Africa),
oh, ravished face of a plagued woman,
junky at 103rd Street station as she slowly turned
into red meat from a Francis Bacon painting,
her body disintegrating, smelling
of Kali, she looked holy like a Queen of Sheba,
her gold lock supporters
and proud lips and nose pointed to heaven,
my feet were weak, I entered the
wet cave of the train,
and I sat down.

East Side Blues Again

Food and money, money and food
what more do you want!
From the top of the World Trade Center—
now you want art? Now you want
pretty pictures! Now you want
to feed your soul with music and dreams
and fleeting emotion when
every second person is black in the New York jails
and in the public schools every other words
is "Tengo mucha hambre," and then
you seek social justice, and then you
think of education so you can learn
that what you earn in a day
equals the average annual income in Ethiopia.

Oh, food and money, money and food,
What more do you want?
But then you think of your body and you remember
mental fitness and all the people who
lack food, money and food.
what more do you want?
There is a magazine we call "Life" in which
Meryl Streep smiles from a cover
wishing everyone Happy New Year and again
she's "on top,"
or almost so...

V
descending
the
'three-jewelled staircase'

LOVE

Love gets up
makes coffee
cooks an omelette…
Love disappears
walks through the park
never waits for me
disregards time
Love smiles, and then the soft breeze of
Spring, balmy shadows of the Mediterranean
sea rushes by…
Love contemplates
the possibility of becoming
a fiery monk in Punjab…
Love hates me
for slipping into the moonlight
and the concrete of 45th Street
Love perseveres,
goes away, sings a song
Love imprisons sunshine in his hair
Love sleeps, visits God
breathes the air
leaves tiny white drops of pain on my back,
thinks of Bali rains, becomes purple,
flies away…
Love murders, spits out venom,
turns to dust, powdered bricks, crumbling mortar,
Love remains, the spirit grows…

On Death

it's almost like you planned
your week and ended up
in an emergency room
you started counting up flowers & days
on your night table
the transfusion & lamp constantly lit
above your head
here to remind you that you've reached
the age of enlightenment
because you finally understood
many basic things but the rotten body
deceived you & knowledge
you learnt dissolved slowly to
a big pink cloud
salmon color right there

Memory on the Line

From certain memories we never recover,
from some we do, but altogether it is not
the same water we crossed once.
From some diseases we get cured, from some
we never recover, the latter keep us
warm and happy
though we should know by now
that happiness is the cure
for non-attachment
and the photograph on which
both of us look
in different directions,
well, that one happened too,
but did I say "directions"?
And did I say "both"?

The Test

When I want to test my friends
I seek advice and ask them: What should I do with
my lover?
They say: Throw him out, change the locks,
tell him you have AIDS, call the police,
beat him up, kiss him softly,
make him a salad, and He says:
I know that I don't know anything,
and then he says:
I think Socrates said the same thing.
I don't think you are Socrates, I say.
I don't think there's need
to test your friends, he says.

On Losing Just About Everything I Own But My Life

How lucky! To be 32
and not in jail and hooked on neither
drugs nor alcohol,
quite by myself, connected to my environment,
slapped by destiny,
still fond of you,
enjoying the calm breeze of Spring,
running along East 5th Street,
still careless, still happy, still free…

On Nothingness

Nothing unusual or inappropriate
about you, and although
making love to you feels like dying,
I wish we could stretch
these tangible points of imagination
a little bit further so this poem
reads like free verse,
this particular poem of mine
conceived by you...

On Impermanence

I
The cats were meowing
the cows were cowing,
horses were neighing, creepy people
playing with evil thoughts and useless fears
—ignorance was vast and evenings quiet,
it was a certain Dharma of the universe
as you and I decided to stand alone
against the trivial, against quotations,
against stale habits,
against the anti, against actions,
against the ordinary, against the unusual,
against our own grain, for the sake of love,
for the sake of life whipping by
like those huge Japanese monsters
unrequited by the lake where
our particular friendship took a walk
like a young maiden who
failed to be raped by the cold
winds of Mount Fuji
which was so pleasant
to gaze at, at times

II
Sometimes you fake friendliness
and sometimes you depart so far away, no
messengers of the Gods of my heart
can reach you, everywhere you go
you maintain the solitary posture
of a warrior from ancient times,
but then you dream
through your fingers and
inside of me you
never depart, perhaps
you are entitled to every folly,
and when you are laughter
I attempt a bluff,
sometimes I trust the elusive and
sometimes the game gets rough

III
Sometimes I dive into your face
and discover mountains and slow valleys
with rivulets of pain running deep
and long caves of uncertainty ---
sometimes you disappear before my eyes
and I can see almost nothing,
the mist of my heart covering my will
with thin perfumed veils,
sometimes I become quiet
like a mute lizard resting beneath
the horrid beauty of your rising sun

Games We Play

Playing games in the moonlight
renders moonlight a certain glamour
what color of light could it be?
When I try to open my oven
to heat the place, certain memories of warmth
are brought back to me—
whose place could this be?
Monkey climbs the tree,
a woman sobs alone in her room,
what tree could it be?
Friends greet each other, feed each other courage,
eat together, laugh—what kind of laughter
could it be?
Confusion arises, eats the heart,
bad taste rules the world—
a law of nature could it be?

The smart grow silent
—a penny for duality—
the loud tell us what to do—
whose perception could it be?
Loyalty brings rewards
but in times of hardship only instincts remain
whose instincts might they be?

INSANE

How is it that the sick
call themselves "the doctors"?
How is it that the crooks
got hold of the divine?

What happened here?
(Haven't I left town only for three months?)
And where did you go last night—I dare
not ask you!
This music sounds strange—haven't I
heard it before?
Haven't I gone insane,
asking all these questions
I've already answered moons ago?

Ancient Verse

While reading the ancient verse
of old masters of poetry
one could find an almost acute
feeling of reverence for nature
and the absolute --- no personal
pronouns used, no dates, no days,
no names to encourage our failed natures, no
Allen Ginsberg to tell me, "We are all bad students,
you know,"
and the foliage, the deep red ocher of the minced
foliage pressed by my feet
under the Bo-tree where
my bound spirit
dwells night and day…

AIRPLANE (on the . . .)

Never will I board a plane again
I don't feel like
insulting the sky all that often
like the other guy
who claimed he was God
and sold me three clouds
and a yellow balloon to go with

Winter Song

Winter is here
as are the homeless and the starving
filling my heart with hope
as I walk up and down
Central Park's condensed crust
and the rest of the poem
is washed away
though some of my poem is to stay…
But dare I say
that the crickets are here also
tonight supporting the lanterns,
luminous shadows of reality, as I descend
the Three-Jewelled staircase
it is so dark all around me,
so predictably silent and unfair…

Brave Song

Oh, smell of oranges in the New York
City subway,
Sufi incense burners,
Eric crying like a mad woman, cold October,
too much sadness, bill collectors threatening
to arrest me, and then—this heavenly music
taking over the 42nd Street station,
when I hear music I always feel divine—
and I always hear music and so I am in heaven,
it comes from eating very little they say,
it comes from bounced checks they say,
but then... this music and this incense
and the smell of oranges—comes from being too thin,
they say,
it comes from studying experimental
theater they say,
it comes from eating too many donuts they say,
it comes from bad lovers who tell
sad stories they say,
it comes from meditating, it comes through gossip,
it comes from nowhere and is nothing, invisible,
and there it stays, jolting me somehow

From Shahnameh Diwan
(after Ferdowsi)

I am a Persian rose,
I am a Sassanian princess,
I am cobalt blue sky,
I am a mountain lioness
I am Abd-al-Aziz's lover
I am a swift gazelle made of wind,
I am a soothing harp.
I am a drop from my father's fountain,
I am a sacred manuscript behind
an illuminated door,
I am a porcelain warrior,
I am formless foam resting
on the winged bull's mouth,
I am a bright saber cutting the day off from the
night,
I am the lightest feather in the Sultan's coronation
turban, I am a gilded gameboard awaiting the
moment
to be lacquered, I am the black lacquer on a
concubine's finger, I am
of red color and transparent background,
when you smile I am,
and I am not
a rose

Poem for All Sentient Beings

Joyful! Practitioner of great Adi Yoga,
happy prisoner of self-discipline who
endures the coldest breaths of
the freezing January air
in the midst of all East Village poverty and beauty,
Joyful! Think of the beings who
were never born, never will be,
or ceased to exist—
to them this poem belongs and not to Carlo
whose sweet sweet voice lifts me up
from all these phenomena and
like the purest oil keeps
my lamp burning in such a dark, murky night

Instinctual

I stopped to write these lines
not knowing
exactly what to think
not knowing
how I felt
about my surroundings and the surrounding
situations—
only this odor
of things I did not like,
among the fir trees, touching
the surface of the fresh mown grass
where I was one
with the sky

Transparency

I don't know who
All these people are
This woman in a courtroom who killed
her husband telling me that she did it
because he was still in love with his first wife
who left their baby five months old at their doorstep
and then she, the stepmother had to bring her up,
take care of her as if she "was her own daughter"
and then the father decided to return
to his child's mother,
and I am wondering: whose circus is this, anyway?
And whose world, which justice applied to us all, and
don't I have
My own worlds to attend to,
Worlds much less complex, deprived and personal,
where advice
Is fed to the birds and where "folly replaces
words such as "Truth" and "Justice"?
Beyond the impossible dwells gray quietness, absence
which becomes
A mode for moods like "let it be" and, "let it go"
Which I hear as I listen to the voices in my skull
Sharp and dull sounds of an outer echo
Which others perceive as a hectic hour…

Rose

O, rose, do you believe in the mystical
fire in your heart!?
Rose, what is the essence of ecstasy
and when does it bleed?
Rose, I see your petals closed tonight, and you seem
worried and disillusioned in your innocence.
you, the eternal one,
lasting but one second
in your divine infinity!

ABOUT THE AUTHOR

Poet, essayist, fiction writer, art critic, and contributing editor to NY Arts from Paris, Nina Zivancevic published her first book of poems *Poems* in 1982 for which she won the National Award in Yugoslavia. She has 9 books of poetry published in Serbian and in English. She also has written three books of short stories and two novels published in Paris, New York and Belgrade: *Recherche Philippe Sollers* (Noel Blandin, 1992), *Inside and Out of Byzantium* (Semiotexte, 1994), and *Vreme Knjige* (Vizantijske Price, 1995). The recipient of three poetry awards, she has edited and participated in numerous anthologies of contemporary world poetry. As editor she has contributed to New York Arts Magazine, American Book Review, East Village Eye (U.S.), Republique de Lettres (Paris), L'Unitá (Italy), Politika and Dnevnik (Yugoslavia).

About Charles Simic

A MacArthur Fellow, a contributor to New York Review of Books, author of more than 30 volumes of poetry, Charles Simic is one of the finest contemporary American poets. Like Zivancevic, he was born in Yugoslavia, but was raised and educated in the U.S. where he lives and teaches at the University of New Hampshire.

About Enzo Cucchi

Enzo Cucchi is a major voice of Italian Transavanguardia. He is and one of the most renowned contemporary artists to emerge on the international scene at the end of the 20th century.

The following works by Enzo Cucchi have been reproduced in this book with the kind permission of the artist and the Bruno Bischofberger Gallery in Zürich, Switzerland.

Ritrattare, page xiv
Lingua d'oro, page 22
Cuore spinoso, page 52
Angelo caduto, page 70 & cover
Abbraccio d'Erba, page 102